Gopher Snakes

A Complete Gopher Snakes Pet Guide

Gopher Snakes General Info, Purchasing, Care, Cost, Keeping, Health, Supplies, Food, Breeding and More Included!

By Lolly Brown

Foreword

Gopher snakes are the kind of pets that are enticingly appealing and quite easy to maintain especially for first time snake keepers. If you're looking for a challenge though or you simply love to take care of such creature then you better do your homework because it's not an easy road when it comes to caring for these wild pets. Gopher snakes are abundant in the wild, and in fact, these snakes are almost always mistaken for a rattlesnake because of many similar body features but according to some owners, Gopher snakes are much more docile compared to rattlesnakes, which makes them quite ideal as pets.

Fortunately, you've bought the right book! You'll learn everything about Gopher snakes including its breed, types, some general information, biological background, origin and distribution, how to maintain it, and also keep it healthy. This book will also delve deeper on how to take care of Gopher snakes in terms of feeding, breeding, habitat requirements as well as its licensing process.

Table of Contents

Introduction

Gopher snakes have six sub – species, and its range includes Indiana, California, and several western states in North America. They measure around 180 to 275 cm depending on the breed (more on this later). Generally, Gopher snakes have huge heads, large eyes but with round pupils, and also quite narrow necks. It has various skin colors like brown, black, yellow, straw, and gray that is either blotched or striped. Its skin color usually blends with its surrounding, and they are usually found in the wild. Gopher snakes also have about 25 to 35 scales, and bear a huge resemblance to rattlesnakes but are not venomous.

When it comes to behavior, these snakes are mostly docile. Some Gopher snakes even lie motionless and are also passive as long as it is handled properly. However, some they can also be quite defensive; they can strike you, hiss loudly or even vibrate its tail if it feels threatened which is why most people mistake it as a rattlesnake, though some Gopher snakes mostly just coils up once handled.

In the next few chapters, you'll learn some general information, and biological background as well as the temperament of Gopher snakes. This book will also delve deeper on how to maintain and keep Gopher snakes in terms of its health, nutrition, habitat and brumation. You will also be informed about its various sub – species and their own physical characteristics as well as its behaviors. The information you'll get to learn in the next few chapters can help you better understand the many kinds of Gopher snakes, and decide which species suits you best.

Gopher snakes appear scary and wild - looking at first but as you get to learn more about it, you'll realize that they can be ideal as pets. Find out why on the next chapter!

Chapter One: Biological Information

Gopher snakes may look like docile and appealing reptiles but it may not be the right choice for everyone. They are large and very powerful creatures which may require a tough keeper so before you decide whether or not it might be the right companion for you and your family, you need to really study what they are and why they behave in a certain way so that you can understand this breed's nature.

In this chapter you will receive an introduction to the breed including some basic biological facts and general information about its sub – species. Find out if you think you can handle the Gopher snakes based on its physical traits, and check out its sub – species to compare their differences.

Taxonomy, Origin and Distribution

Gopher Snakes have a scientific name of *Pituophis catenifer catenifer*. They belong in Kingdom *Animalia*, Phylum *Chordata*, Class *Reptilia*, Order *Squamata*, Family *Colubridae*, Genus *Pituophis*, and Species *P. catenifer*.

As mentioned earlier, Gopher snakes are mostly distributed in North America but they are also abundant in Mexico and even in Canada. These snakes are semi – arboreal, ground dwellers and burrowers. During autumn and winter seasons, these snakes hibernate especially in countries with cold climates. In places with hot temperature like California, these snakes are pretty stable all year round and do not hibernate at all, unless need be. They also have dorsal scales that are keeled on the back, these chain bearing color patterns refers to their scientific name "catenifer." They gain the name "Gopher snakes" because they primarily eat gophers, which are small rodents found underground.

Gopher snakes occur in lowlands, shrublands, woodlands, desert, coniferous forest, farmland, marshes, coastal grasslands, and also prairies.

Size, Life Span, and Physical Appearance

Gopher snakes measures about 4 feet long on average though it can reach up to 7 feet in length. When you first spot a gopher snake, you'll notice a bunch of brown or reddish color blotches on its back, and its ground color is yellow, straw, tan or cream color. There are also smaller blotches found on its side. A dark strip runs in front of its eye to the angle of its jaw.

The Gopher snake also has the ability to unhinge its jaw in order to swallow larger prey. When threatened the Gopher snake prepares for a striking position by lowering its head, hissing loudly, and shaking its tail. This defensive behavior along with its body markings frequently caused the Gopher snake to be mistaken for a Rattlesnake. Their main difference is the tail; Gopher snake tail's has no "rattle," lacks facial pit, and has round pupils.

Gopher snakes are active mainly during the day except in extreme heat when it ventures out at night. Like most reptiles, Gopher snakes are carnivores, and they mostly consume mammals especially in the wild. They feed on animals like rodents particularly gophers, squirrels, rats, rabbits, birds (including its eggs) etc. The Gopher snakes also helps in maintaining the balance in the animal kingdom and the ecosystem as a whole.

These heterothermic creatures have an average lifespan of 12 to 15 years, and its longest recorded life expectancy is 33 years.

Sub – Species of Gopher Snakes

Below are five of the most popular and major kinds of Gopher snakes. Check out its physical and behavioral traits to find out which one is most suitable for you:

Pituophis catenifer affinis – Sonoran Gopher Snake

Distribution: west Texas, southeast California, Sonoran Desert, Mexico

Physical characteristics:

Length: 4 ft. – 7 ft. in length

Body: Has reddish – brown dorsal blotches in its saddle; has darkish brown or black colors on its tail

Behavior and Nature: Sonoran Gopher snakes are relatively aggressive in the wild, but in captivity they can be quite docile. Loves dry deserts wherein they can burrow their heads, and eat the rodents they find underground.

Pituophis catenifer annectens – San Diego Gopher Snake

Distribution: San Diego, Santa Barbara, Baja California, North Mexico, and Catalina Island

Physical characteristics:

Length: 4 ft. – 5 ft. in length

Body: A huge snake with lots of keeled scales; its head is wider than the neck, and has a rounded snout. Its body color can either be tan, yellow, or brown. Has brownish or blackish patterns on its sides, and has a dark stripe in its jaws.

Behavior and Nature: San Diego Gopher snakes are active during the day. They are usually seen on the roads and trails particularly when they are seeking a mate. It is also a good burrower and swimmer.

Pituophis catenifer catenifer – Pacific Gopher Snake

Distribution: Oregon, southern California, Santa Barbara, Sierra Nevada, Tehachapi Mountains, Solano, Napa Counties

Physical characteristics:

Length: 135 – 150 cm in length

Body: Its body has no blotches, but it has stripes with a tan or straw ground color. Its underside is cream in color or sometimes has a yellowish marking with dark spots.

Behavior and Nature: Like most Gopher snakes subspecies, Pacific Gopher Snakes are also non – venomous, and they are quite active at dusk compared to other types of Gopher snakes. However, they can be nocturnal especially during hot seasons. They also prefer to live in dense forests, meadows, farmlands and fields.

Pituophis catenifer deserticola – Great Basin Gopher Snake

Distribution: Arizona, California, Canada, Idaho, Las Vegas, New Mexico, Oregon, Utah, Washington and Wyoming.

Physical characteristics:

Length: 4.5 – 5.75 ft. in length

Body: Great Basin Gopher snakes have dorsal markings that are dark brown or black in color. Its scales are keeled and have a pointed head.

Behavior and Nature: Great Basin Gophers are very good in swimming and climbing. They also prefer living in dry areas like deserts, grasslands, woodlands, riparian areas, and farmlands.

Pituophis catenifer sayi – Bullsnake

Distribution: Central and Northern Mexico, Saskatchewan and Alberta Canada, Northern America

Physical characteristics:

Length: 36 – 84 inches in length

Body: Bull snakes have brownish or yellowish dorsal blotches, and typically have smaller dark spots on its side, its head is also narrow.

Behavior and Nature: Bull snakes coils and puff its body if it as a defense mechanism. It also mimics a rattlesnake when striking; they strike with their mouths closed.

Quick Facts

Distribution and Range: North America, Canada, and Mexico.

Breed Size: long and large – size breed

Body Type and Appearance: Has big eyes with rounded pupils with a large head but narrow necks. Usually have dark stripes on top of its head

Length: between 36 – 96 inches in length depending on the species.

Skin Texture: scaly or has keeled scales

Color: Depends on the species, and their environment; has cream, brown with dark blotches or has a yellow, straw, tan, reddish ground color.

Temperament: docile and non – venomous but can be aggressive when threatened.

Diet: Gophers or rodents, birds, rats, rabbits, squirrel, and mostly wild mammals found in the forest.

Habitat: Woodlands, Grasslands, Dry Forests, Deserts, Meadows, Marshes, Fields. Mostly dry areas with a warm climate.

Health Conditions: generally healthy but predisposed to common illnesses such as anorexia, vomiting or regurgitation, acariasis, and Pneumonia

Lifespan: average 12 to 15 years; 33 years is the longest recorded life expectancy of a Gopher snake.

Chapter Two: Gopher Snakes as Pets

Now that you have a basic idea about what Gopher snakes are all about, and have a background knowledge about its popular sub – species, it's time to get to know Gopher snakes even more in this chapter. This time though, we will delve deeper on what it takes to really become a keeper by learning about its temperament as well as the license or permit needed for keeping them, and also the budget you'll most probably need to provide all its requirements. These are all important before you purchase a Gopher snake as your pet. You, as a potential keeper need to make sure that your pet snake is safe, secure, and happy.

What Makes It a Great Pet

Gopher snakes only comes second to Ball Pythons and Corn Snakes in terms of having them as pets. However, they are equally ideal even if they are quite large and powerful. One of the biggest hurdles to getting a pet snake is convincing your housemates, especially if you live with your parents. The idea of keeping a snake at home is difficult to sell. To one who is not used to snakes, having one at home can be terrifying, especially if they have a phobia of snakes.

In this section, we will give you some tips on how to persuade anyone in your house to let you have a pet snake and assure them that it is safe and family – friendly.

- **Keep Calm and Don't Rush.** You shouldn't suddenly tell your family that you'll be getting a pet snake. Learn to wait until you have familiarized them enough with snakes so that they'll be comfortable enough to entertain the idea of living with one. You should also be able to answer their questions about Gopher snakes like the benefits of taking care of one, how much it will cost, and how big it will get. Be honest so that they will be able to assess the risks and costs of living with a pet snake.

- **Get guidebooks, show videos, and tell them about the breeders or reptile owners who keep snakes.** Show them how easy it is to maintain and take care of a Gopher snake; tell them about how other owners are having fun keeping snakes as pets so your family or roommate will know that they do not have to be afraid. You can also familiarize them with snakes by showing YouTube videos or going with them to the zoo.

- **Share what you know about Gopher snakes and familiarize your family with them.** Since you now know some basic facts about the Gopher snake why not tell your family or housemates about them? As previously mentioned it is non – venomous, docile, very friendly, has different colors, and doesn't get too large and thick like a python. These will come in handy when you ask your housemates or parents if they will be okay with you keeping a Gopher snake.

- **Assure them that you are going to be a responsible keeper.** As with all pets, you must be able to take care of your Gopher snake. You should have enough time to spend with your snake. Assure your relatives or housemates that you are responsible enough to keep your snake, and that they won't end up having to feed it for you or fight it off, if it escapes and becomes agitated. This can only be done by showing them, not just telling them, that you are a responsible keeper.

- **Never ever force your family or housemates to accept your potential pet snake.** If you've tried everything you can to convince your parents or roommates but they still don't want to live with a snake, don't force them to. Even if Gopher snakes aren't venomous, people who aren't prepared to live with one may in some way agitate it. Even worse, it may cause a fight between you and your housemates.

- **Wait until you can get your own place or find housemates willing to accommodate your Gopher snake.** It's not easy to convince people to live with a snake, but there is reason for them to be scared. Despite everything, snakes are not used to people, and people are almost taught to fear snakes. So don't push it – wait until you can get your own place. Before you get your own Gopher snake, you must make sure the people you live with are okay with it, if you can't find anyone willing to support you either your roommates or family members, it is better not to take care of one at least in the meantime. Otherwise, you might end up having to relocate it – and Gopher snakes aren't easy to put up for adoption or just give to anyone.

Temperament and Behavioral Characteristics with other Pets

There are certain qualities that make them maybe even better than other snake species particularly its temperament. In this chapter we'll find out what makes Gopher snakes a good pet choice for you.

As mentioned in the previous chapter, Gopher snakes are generally docile species, but for some of its sub – species they tend to become aggressive when threatened, especially if you caught it in the wild or have not had proper socialization and taming. Gopher snakes are very active during day time and are also very curious of its surrounding which is why you need to provide adequate space for it to freely move around. Some owners love to keep Gopher snakes more than other snake species because it's very easy to feed. It usually doesn't turn down any food, or maybe if it does, it's only a handful.

When it comes to handling them, domesticated Gopher snakes are generally easy to tame, and are reluctant to bite provided that you make them feel secure and you don't trigger them to defend themselves. Since Gopher snakes can grow quite large, long and heavy, it's not advisable for families with very young children. But of course, you can still keep one provided that you keep these snakes out of your children's reach. Nevertheless, for those friends or neighbors that are curious yet courageous on how to handle snakes, a Gopher snake is one of the best snake species to hold because it's very tame and docile. It's best to handle such species while they're still young so that they'll get used to being touch.

All reptile and snake species for this matter are carnivorous and natural predators. Gopher snakes may have good temperament and docile to people but when it comes to other animals particularly smaller species, their basic animal instinct will apply, so if you don't want to get your other household pets eaten, make sure that you keep them away from your pet snake or provide a secured enclosure so that your Gopher will not slip away.

Usually Gopher snakes will not be a threat to other pets such as cats or dogs – as long as you don't let your pet snake loose around the house, otherwise that will be a different story.

Pros and Cons of Gopher Snakes

Pros

- They are non – venomous snakes
- Suited for novice keepers or beginners

- Generally docile and easy to tame, curious and active.
- Safe around people provided that there is supervision and they are properly handled, though some Gopher snake species may tend to be much aggressive.
- Very easy to feed, does not neglect any food compared to other snake species.
- Relatively cheap to buy and the overall cost is not that expensive.
- Unlikely to get ill with appropriate care.
- Trouble-free feeding and shedding in captivity.
- Can live for about 12 to 15 years
- Requires no supervision, provided that its enclosure is safe and secured.

Cons

- Some sub – species like the Sonora Gopher snake and/or Bull Snakes are quite aggressive, and may not be ideal as pets, though some owners have properly tamed it.

- Not as receptive to humans as other animals usually kept as pets like cats or dogs.

- Growth may be quite hard to manage since it can get as long as 7 feet.

- Cannot be trained compared to other household pets, although socialization may help.

- May not be ideal for families with very young children

- Its food may only be available in reptile shops or major pet stores

- Can live up to 15 years so they may be difficult to rehome.

- Not for the faint – hearted or for those who can't stand snakes.

FAQs about Snake Licensing

Do I need a license or permit to keep my Gopher Snakes?

The answer is yes and no. You don't need a license to keep Gopher snakes since they are non – venomous which means that even if they bite a human or a stranger, it will not kill them. Yes because it also depends on which country, state or region you live. License may not be required but permits are most likely needed. Make sure that you ask first your local and state laws and an ordinance, to see what is permitted and what is not.

What are examples of documents that I need to keep a Gopher snake legally?

Again, this highly depends on your local state, region or even your apartment building. Some places may ban keeping reptile pets such as snakes, some may need permits. The most common requirements to keep your snake legally are things like pet insurance, micro-chipping, medical history or proof of medical checkups from your vet, proof that you acquire the snake from a legit and/or recognized breeder and that it is bred in captivity – and not just caught in the wild as well as your other identification documents.

Why should I acquire license for my Gopher snake?

Well, not only because the law may require it but also because for legal purpose. Imagine if for some reason, your pet slipped away and have been found by other people and they have reported it to authorities. It can be returned to you but of course, they will first ask your permit/license to make sure that you are keeping this animal legally. If they found out that you don't, your pet may not be returned to you or worse you might even get fined for it. Vets may also reject your pet if they found out that you are not keeping it legally.

What if I want to travel and bring my pet snake with me?

This is why licenses and/or permits are important. It is necessary for importing, exporting, or traveling with an exotic or a naturally dangerous animal. Obviously, there may be special laws about bringing your pet with you to other countries especially in United Kingdom or Asia. Make sure to research thoroughly about how to bring your pet snake to another country, and the specific laws that apply depending on what part of the region or place you will stay. Also make sure to check the rules of the airline and/or ships that you'll get on board about bringing exotic pets like snakes.

Cost of Owning a Snake

In this section you will receive an overview of the expenses associated with purchasing and keeping snakes as pets such as food, maintenance supplies, enclosures, veterinary care, and other essential costs so that you can manage your budget before you acquire one.

Keeping pets in general can be costly, and even if these snakes are low maintenance and quite inexpensive compared to other breed, you will still need to provide its supplies to maintain a healthy lifestyle and adequate environment for your pet.

These things will definitely add up to your daily budget, and the cost will vary depending on where you purchase it; the size of the enclosure, the nutrients included in its food, the equipment needed for proper maintenance, the time being etc. If you want to seriously own a Gopher snake as a pet you should be able to cover the necessary costs it entails. The initial expenses associated with keeping Gopher snakes as pets include the cost of the breed itself as well as the its substrate, accessories, initial medical checkups, micro-chipping, licensing, food, and other equipment needed. Find out the things you need to buy on the next section.

Before you even buy or bring home your Gopher snake, you have to make sure that you get all your basic supplies ready. The first thing to do is set up its habitat, and depending on the kind of Gopher snake you're going to buy, you may opt for a 20 – gallon enclosure (glass vivarium is preferred) for baby Gopher snakes, of course you may need to buy a relatively larger enclosure if you will acquire a fully

– grown snake already. The rule of thumb is that they should be able to fully stretch out inside its cage. Make sure that you also buy a secure screen top so that your Gopher will not be able to escape.

The next thing you should buy is a substrate which will function as your snake's bedding. It's highly recommended that you buy aspen shadings, reptile bar or coconut fiber so that your pet will get easily comfortable with its new habitat.

You should also provide a cozy hiding place that is large enough for your Gopher snake to coil up inside whenever he feels like it. You can also purchase some cage furniture or décor to make the enclosure aesthetically appealing, although don't put too much so that that your pet can have enough space. You should also keep in mind to never put any outdoor stuff because it can harm your pet or may be toxic for them. Aside from substrate, and a hiding place, you should also purchase a relatively large water dish to give your Gopher snake a place to soak, and also help increase humidity.

Snakes are cold – blooded animals, which is why you should also provide him a heat source. You need to purchase a basking lamp, and an undertank heater as well as gauges to regulate temperature and humidity levels to keep your snake at a proper temperature.

Aside from all of these, you should also buy another smaller feeding tank/enclosure, and stock up some frozen rodents before your new pet moves in. Using a separate tank is a great way for your snake to not associate your hand or the habitat being open for feeding time.

Your pet's food are primarily rodents or other similar species (more on this later) which you can buy based on your snake's age and size. On average, an adult snake eats 5 rodents or more in a month. You may prefer to shop at local pet stores – which may cost you more but are convenient. Online, buying in bulk may cost you less though there will also be shipping fees.

When it comes to vet bills or medical checkups, your Gopher snake will not need a lot of visits to the vet – however, you still have to take it to the vet for a routine check-up every once in a while to make sure it is healthy. Getting a Gopher snake checked may cost you around $75 or more. You should also set aside enough money for any emergency cases, even if Gopher snakes aren't venomous; paying for the medical cost of a snake bite still isn't cheap. While Gopher snakes are usually docile, you still have to consider the risk of you or someone else being bitten.

Licensing and acquiring permits or micro-chipping your pet will also cost you a few dollars annually depending on your location. Last but not least is the cost of the Gopher snake itself. A Gopher snake species from a reputable breeder will cost between $50 and $69, it may even be cheaper if you acquire it from a backyard breeder, although make sure that it is healthy, and they are keeping it legally.

Cost of Keeping a Gopher Snake:

- Gopher Snake breed: $50 - $69
- Glass Enclosure with a screen top or lid: approx. $100 (depending on size)
- Bedding or Substrate: $10
- Water Dish: $10 - $15 (depending on size/quality)
- Under Tank Heater: $25 or more
- Basking Lamp: $30 or more
- Heat and Water Temperature Regulator/ Gauges: $5 or more (often comes with the under tank heater/basking lamp)
- Hiding Place: $5 - $10
- Feeding tank: $30 - $50 or more
- Food: $10 - $15 (depending on brand and amount)
- Vet bills: $75 or more
- License/Permit: depends on the state/countery you live in.

Chapter Three: Purchasing and Selecting a Healthy Breed

Once you have set up and prepare your potential Gopher snake's habitat, it's now time for the fun part! In this chapter you will be provided with the criteria on selecting a healthy Gopher snake breed as well as a reputable and trustworthy snake breeder. You will also learn where to legally purchase a snake breed. It's essential that before you purchase any snake for this matter, you should first consider on who bred and raised them and how they are being taken care of, especially if you'd prefer purchasing a juvenile snake or an adult Gopher. You'll also be provided with links where you can purchase a snake online. Keep in mind that purchasing a healthy breed is one of the most essential things that every potential snake keeper should learn about.

Where to Purchase an Gopher Snake Breed

This section will discuss the different places where you can purchase your own Gopher snake as well as some tips on how to avoid bad or illegal snake breeders.

Reptile Shops

Reptile shops are highly recommended among expert and novice snake keepers including reptile enthusiasts and veterinarians. What makes it great is that, you can go in there and ask any questions about your chosen breed. The staffs are usually very helpful and are experts when it comes to any snake species given the time they have spent with a lot of breeds. You can also find a variety of species for a particular breed even snake species that may not be available in a standard commercial pet store, which is good because you want to have as many Gopher snake choices as possible.

Private Breeders

Private breeders are the people who breed, raise, and keep snakes for the love of it! It's another great source because these people don't just breed snakes because they want to sell their pets, they do it because they just actually care for these pet species which is a great sign because it means that you're getting a snake breed that is well – taken care of, and eliminates many unwanted factors when it comes to finding a reputable breeder. But of course, you also have to be careful when it comes to dealing with private breeders, make sure to do you due diligence, and ask the right questions to spot a good breeder from a bad breeder.

Reptile Shows

Reptile shows is another great place to buy a snake because every species that they sell is always much cheaper than pet shops and even private breeders. You can buy a healthy Gopher snake that is cheaper than what they are usually worth which is fantastic because you'll save a lot of money, though you also need to be careful, and make sure that the people you're buying from knows what they're doing.

Rescue Centers

If you choose to become a season keeper or someone who maybe just want to try keeping a snake but don't necessarily see yourself raising them for a long time, then you might want to acquire your snake from rescue centers. You can do this by checking your local rescue center.

However, the availability of a particular snake species like Gopher snakes will vary; you may not have a lot of choices when it comes to selecting a healthy breed or sometimes may not have any choice at all. Some rescue centers offer certain snake species for free or for just a minimal amount but you may need to prove to them that you'll be a good and responsible breeder. Breeders love to support rescue centers because they're the ones who are saving these species' lives, and picking up after the bad keepers.

How to Spot a Good Snake Breeder

Now that you have an idea on where to purchase your snake, it's time to determine who to buy it from. Selecting a breeder is the first step before you buy any pet because if the breeder is reputable, caring, and a responsible caregiver, you can be sure that the snake is well – taken care of. Here are the following guidelines for you to be able to choose a reputable snake breeder:

- Good breeders must be knowledgeable about the breeds they raise, and should give you specific info about the breed.

- They have to take note that the primary reason for breeding a snake is for health or because it is their hobby, and not just for appearance or selling purposes.

- They should be able to teach you how to properly set up the enclosure, where to place it, and the right temperature/humidity levels needed.

- Good breeders tend to know a lot about the species they breed, so they often can supply more information than a typical pet store clerk. If they only tell you general information, chances are they're not really interested with their pets.

- Good breeders know how to establish a good relationship with their potential/existing buyers. Be sure to ask for referrals from their previous buyers so that you can ask them about the pet they've bought from this breeder, and if they have good rapport.

- A good breeder who is passionate about the animals that they breed will want to talk to you about them. They will not hesitate to answer your questions and at the same time ask questions of their own. If a breeder doesn't bother to answer all of your questions in order to get you to spend money with them in the first place, chances are that they will be unresponsive to you after the sale.

- Good breeders will walk you through every step of the process. They are willing to answer all of your questions and if they think that you are not a good fit as an owner, they won't sell it to you. Yes, they want to earn money but they also want to protect the integrity of the hobby. That's usually a great sign that the breeder really care about the pets.

Some Questions You Can Ask to Spot a Good Breeder

- Can you tell me information about Gopher snakes or this particular breed?

- What are the things I need for its habitat? Any stores or brands you can refer? What kind of enclosure does it prefer?

- How did you breed the snakes? How did you raise them?

- How many times should I feed it? How often? What food or brands can you recommend?

- How do I set up its habitat? What should be the temperature?

- How many years have you been in business, and what kind of experience do you have as a breeder?

- What do you specialize in? What types of species do you breed and sell?

- Do you offer any kind of a warranty or guarantee? If so, how long?

- Can I ask any referrals?

Characteristics of a Healthy Breed

Whether you choose a baby Gopher, juvenile or an adult, there are several things to keep in mind when selecting a healthy breed.

The first you should look out for is the eyes; you want to look for clear eyes that are free of any discharge or cloudiness except of course, when the snake is preparing to shed. Next is the breathing; you need to look out for a healthy breathing with no signs of labor breathing, and no nostril discharge. You should also opt to get a snake that has a rounded and full body, and a species that is active and alert to its environment. It should not have any mobility issues, the snake should be able to move freely as well.

Never purchase or acquire a snake that has blisters on its skin or a snake that has a smooth and supple skin because these are signs of ill health. Another sign to watch out for is raised scales because it usually indicates that the snake is infected with mites. The ventral opening should always be indistinguishable on the underside, and there should be no discharge coming from its anus. The snake should readily use its tongue to smell and search its environment. When you lift it up, you should be able to feel a sense of strength to its body.

It's also highly recommended that you choose a Gopher snake that is bred in captivity, because wild Gopher snakes may carry with them health problems and parasites. They are also harder to handle since they have lived in the wild all their life, and are not used to handling or socialization.

List of Breeders and Rescue Websites

While going to a reptile pet shop or rescue center is convenient, going online to buy your Gopher snake may save you some money. If you want to see your chosen snake up close and personal, however, you may want to opt for local breeders in your area, speak to other snake breeders or try looking for reptile or Gopher snake groups. The people in these groups are usually knowledgeable about reptiles and snakes, and may give you good advice on where to get your Gopher snake. You can also try visiting snake forums online to ask for advice.

Here is the list of breeders and adoption rescue websites around United States and United Kingdom:

United States Breeders and Rescue Websites

Back Water Reptiles
<http://www.backwaterreptiles.com/snakes/gopher-snake-for-sale.html>

Kingsnake.com
<http://market.kingsnake.com/index.php?cat=98>

Underground Reptiles
<https://undergroundreptiles.com/product-category/animals/snakes/garter-gopher-bull-amp-pine-snakes/>

Big Apple Herp

<http://www.bigappleherp.com/ANIMALS-LIVE-REPTILES/Pine-Snakes-Gopher-Snakes>

California Herps

<http://www.californiaherps.com/snakes/pages/p.c.catenifer.html>

First Choice Reptiles

<http://www.firstchoicereptiles.com/gopher-snake-for-sale/>

SPSnakes.com

<http://www.spsnakes.com/snakes.htm>

Snake Museum

<http://www.snakemuseum.com/58-bulls-pines-gophers>

Mount Pleasure Herps

<http://www.mtpleasantherps.com/gopher-snakes-for-sale---mt-pleasant-herps.html>

Sacramento Splash Rescue

<https://www.sacsplash.org/blog-entry/great-gopher-snake-rescue>

J & R Reptile Rescue

<http://jrreptilerescue.tripod.com/>

Adopt – a – Pet

<http://www.adoptapet.com/s/snake-adoption>

Snake Are Us Rescue

<http://www.snakesareus.com/>

Idaho Wild Life Rescue

<http://idahowildliferescue.org/bullsnake-aka-gopher-snake/>

Sonoma Country Reptile Rescue

<http://www.sonomacountyreptilerescue.com/native_species/pituophis_catenifer.html>

Snake Busters

<http://www.snakebusters.com/>

United Kingdom Breeders and Rescue Websites

HD – Reptiles UK

<https://www.hd-reptiles.co.uk/reptile-room/our-breeding-room/bulls-pines-and-gopher-snakes/>

Exotic – Pets UK

<https://www.exotic-pets.co.uk/snakes-for-sale.html>

Wharf Aquatics UK

<http://www.wharfaquatics.co.uk/reptilestocksnakes.htm>

NewsNow UK

<http://www.newsnow.co.uk/classifieds/pets-animals/gopher-snakes-for-sale.html

Reptiles Plus UK

<http://www.reptilesplus.co.uk/stocklist/snakes.php>

Paws For Thought

<http://www.pawsforthought.co.uk/snakes-for-sale-leeds>

Mansfield Aquatic, Reptile & Pet Center

<http://www.marpc.co.uk/html/other-snakes.html>

Exeter Exotics

<http://www.exeterexotics.co.uk/snake-other.html>

BHB Reptiles

<https://www.bhbreptiles.com/>

Preloved UK

<http://www.preloved.co.uk/classifieds/pets/reptiles/all/uk/gopher+snakes>

Reptilia Reptile Rescue

<http://reptiliareptilerescue.co.uk/index.html>

Snake Busters

<http://www.snakebusters.com/>

Proteus Reptile Trust Rescue

<http://www.proteusreptiletrust.org/>

RSCPA Reptile Rescue

<http://www.rspcareptilerescue.co.uk/>

North East Reptile Rescue

<http://nerr.co.uk/>

Chapter Four: Habitat Requirements for Gopher Snakes

Setting up your pet snake's cage or enclosure is not as hard as it may seem. You just need to buy a couple of things as previously mentioned, and know where to put those things properly. This chapter will teach you the step by step process on how you can properly set up your Gopher snake's enclosure, the functions of each material, and the proper temperature to keep your cold – blooded buddy warm and comfortable in his new surroundings. This chapter will also cover some tips on how to maintain cleanliness in your pet's enclosure.

How to Set Up Your Snake's Enclosure

The first thing you need in setting up your pet snake's new environment is its glass terrarium. As mentioned earlier, you can purchase a 20 – gallon tank for your Gopher snake or maybe something a little bit bigger especially if you bought an adult Gopher snake which is relatively longer and larger than baby or juvenile snakes. Since Gopher snakes are quite active pets who love to explore and naturally enjoy living in dry areas, you should make sure that you somewhat replicate that kind of environment so that it will be able to adjust pretty easily.

The second thing you need to decide before proceeding in decorating your pet snake is the hot side and the normal side of the enclosure. We will delve on this later regarding on why you'll need to provide ample space and the proper temperature, but it's important that you assign a space for a basking area, and a space for a normal temperature where your snake can rest and coil up so that you'll know where to properly put the materials you bought.

The third most important thing you should provide inside a cage is the bedding and/or substrate. You can use shredded Aspen bedding for North American snake species because it gives a nice and thick layer of bedding which is perfect for your pet Gopher snake since these snake species loves to burrow, and just pretty much love to go through the bedding. Think of the bedding as one huge hiding spot for your snake, when you have a thick layer, your Gopher snake will really be happy burrowing themselves in the entire bottom of your cage, and they will also feel secure. Another advantage of Aspen bedding is that it's very easy to clean, and the cage will also be easy to spot clean. If ever you need to add moisture during your snake's shedding, the Aspen will hold moisture well – enough to help them aid in the shedding but not get so damped and soggy that it's going to stay too wet.

Next thing you need to do is place the cage materials like water bowls/water dish, some plants, perches, and your snake's hiding spot but before you do make sure to determine the right size you'll need for your pet. Aside from the things mentioned, you can also add other materials like jungle vine and bamboo bars where your snake can climb up and perch. However, make sure that it is suitable for your snake species. Since Gopher snakes are semi – arboreal animals, they may prefer these types of materials because it closely resembles tree branches or vines, though you can opt to just purchase simple but thicker and perhaps smaller tree branches especially for baby Gopher snakes.

You can also buy a basic hiding spot that will fit the size of your pet, these are very practical, and cheap but may look dull. If you want to make your enclosure aesthetically appealing, you can choose to use habba huts, turtle hides, rock outcrops hides, skull or crystal snake caves, reptishelters and the likes. It all comes in various shapes, colors and sizes so it's up to you to decide which will be perfect for your pet and the kind of décor you want to have. The only thing you need to keep in mind, especially if you own a baby snake is that you don't want to purchase a hiding spot that is too big. Baby snakes will want something that will make them feel nice, safe and secure like in a small dark hiding spot. They prefer to feel covered and contained in all sides because it makes them feel better and not too exposed compared to when you put them in hiding spots that are too large for their size.

Aside from hiding spots, you can also stack a few sticks of branches, and cork flaps. Cork flaps provide a nice snug when you lay it flat on the bedding, and it also creates another hiding spot for your pet snake. You can also grab a few mosses and fresh or plastic leaves to add decoration in your cage, which also mimics the sort of wild natural surroundings that snakes love.

Another great technique to make sure that your snake utilizes all the hiding spots, caves or branches you purchase is to kind of bury it halfway through the substrate and not just place it on top of the bedding so that your snake doesn't necessarily have to come out of the burrow to use it.

Once you've set up all the materials needed inside the cage, you then need to set up the under tank heater, the basking lamp, and also attach a heat and humidity gauges.

Regulating Temperature

You should put the heat pad or under tank heater on the basking area's side of the cage at the bottom to give your snake a warm spot. The temperature for Gopher snakes should be 85 – 90 degrees Fahrenheit. Next is the basking lamp or overheat lamp that has like a UVB light, put it on top of the cage's lid or on the side to help warm up that side of the cage especially during cold season. During warmer season, you don't actually need to light it up; you can just put a dimmer on the lamp to turn down the light a bit.

Remember that the basking area should cover about less than half of the cage, and the cooler side should have a temperature that is less than 80 degrees Fahrenheit. Water bowls should also be located on the cooler side and not on the basking area.

The next thing is to attach an analog thermometer to regulate the cage's temperature. You may want to put the thermometer close to the substrate or the hiding spot of your snake. Since some thermometers are easy to remove, you can use the same thing to check the temperature on the cooler side every now and then, especially during summer. Make sure to monitor temperatures come summer time when everything is a lot warmer.

Chapter Five: Nutrition and Feeding

In this chapter, you'll learn the majority of your pet snake's nutritional needs, feeding guidelines, as well as feeding amount and frequency. Proper nutrition will go a long way for your snake's health and growth. Feeding your Gopher snake is not that complicated but you have to make sure that its level of activity, age, and body should be taken into consideration to meet its nutritional diet needs. Gopher snakes should be given the right amount of recommended food for a balanced nutrition because proper diet can lengthen the life expectancy of your snake and also protect them from serious illnesses.

Nutritional Needs of Gopher Snakes

Gopher snakes are one of the best snake species to feed because they don't neglect the food brought to them most of the time compared to other snake species. As mentioned previous chapters, Gopher snakes are mainly carnivores who likes to eat mammals particularly gophers, squirrels, rodents, rabbits and birds found in the forest and underneath the ground, of course you can't really sustain that kind of diet since they are in captivity so the best food you can feed them are fuzzies or thawed mice which are frozen and easy to buy, though you may need to serve it a bit warm to your snake. You can do this by putting these frozen fuzzies on a sealed plastic, and kind of heat it with lukewarm water before feeding it to your Gopher snake. You should also avoid feeding your Gopher snake a wild-caught prey because this can transmit parasites.

Gopher snakes like to constrict their prey in the wild to kill them, but feeding them a live mice or rat is highly discouraged because it can cause damage to your pet. Aside from that you can also feed your snake every now and then with small quail or dove eggs as a treat. You do not need to supplement your Gopher snake's meals with vitamin powders or similar products. Gopher snakes can get all the vitamins and minerals that they need from the food that you feed them, without the need to add anything.

Many people who own snakes insist that their pets need the thrill of hunting and catching live prey, such as mice and rats. This is definitely not true. Physical and mental stimulation comes from the overall environment that you create for your Gopher snake, and not from attempting to catch a live prey in a small space. Live preys can be too active for your baby Gopher snake because there is a large possibility that live prey can attack your Gopher snake, which could result your pet to become frightened of it, and it can be very difficult to feed him from them on. Attacks that come from live prey can permanently scar and disfigure your Gopher snake.

Therefore, feeding your snake a pre-killed prey is safer. The kind of prey you're feeding your Gopher snake will determine how serious an attack it can potentially cause. If you like to feed your Gopher snakes a live prey, it is recommended that you provide a food source for the prey so it will not try to eat your snake. You have to watch it closely for any signs that it may be gnawing or biting your snake. If ever this will happen, remove the prey immediately and take your Gopher snake to the veterinarian.

Remember, the threats that a live prey animal present can be completely eliminated by just feeding pre-killed prey instead. Pre-killed prey can be bought live and then you can just kill it, or you can buy it already killed. You can freeze pre-killed prey for up to six months. Just be sure to thaw it thoroughly and warm it to slightly above room temperature before feeding it to your Gopher snake.

Feeding Conditions

The first thing you need to consider to make sure that your Gopher snakes eat properly is to maintain and set up its habitat correctly. Gopher snakes have its own unique habitat requirements referring to lighting, temperature, humidity, layout, accessories, size of the habitat, and more. Gopher snakes that are in an environment that is too dark, too cold, too small or else improperly maintained will most probably have a decrease in appetite and may eventually refuse food completely. Be sure to set up and stabilize their habitat before bringing your Gopher snake home so they can also digest and absorb food properly.

When it comes to feeding your Gopher snakes, a separate feeding enclosure may not be a requirement in some cases, but it can definitely be helpful. Using a different environment for feeding times can maintain the main enclosure cleaner and more sanitary. A separate feeding enclosure is recommended.

Feeding Amount and Frequency

Even if Gopher snakes grow into a relatively large and long snake, they only need to be fed about once a week or in ten days. You can choose to feed your adult Gopher snake with a squirrel that is about the size of the rodent. Make sure to not attempt to feed your snake too often otherwise it may cause digestive problems or your snake will most likely not eat if it isn't hungry.

How to Feed Your Gopher Snake

- If you feed your Gopher Snake, don't handle it for at least 24 hours after feeding the snake. Give them time to digest their food because it is not a good idea if you handle it straight after you feed it.

- You should always take note that fresh water in a shallow dish must always be available.

- Take into account of using tongs when feeding your Gopher snake to avoid accidental bites.

- When preparing a pre-killed prey for your pet, thaw it by running it under warm water.

- Increase the size of the rodent appropriately as your snake grows. A recommended sized meal is one that is no bigger than the width of the snake's body, or leaves only a small lump in the snake's body after being consumed.

- Be aware that your Gopher snake can get injured or can sometimes die from prey injuries and bites.

- When you feed them, feed it out of its enclosure so that when you put your hand on the snake's cage, it won't think that your hand is a food thus, preventing to be bitten by your snake.

Chapter Six: Maintenance for Gopher Snakes

Part of your snake's husbandry is the maintenance of their habitat. Providing them with all the materials they need to replicate their environment in the wilderness is a great way of caring for them but you also have to make sure that you maintain it by thoroughly cleaning their enclosure so that they can have a decent and sanitary place to live in. A great and clean environment plus proper feeding will make them happy pets. In this chapter you'll learn some tips on how keep their enclosures clean and appealing as well as some caring tips. You'll also get to learn how to snake – proof your home.

Spot Cleaning Your Snake's Enclosure

Spot cleaning means that you thoroughly clean not just the cage of your snake but also all the materials you placed inside the cage. You need to clean your Gopher snake's habitat enclosure regularly as well. The humidity within the enclosure can be a perfect breeding ground for the growth of bacteria. Most reptiles can be prone to skin and bacterial infection if left alone in unclean surroundings for long which is why regular cage maintenance and cleaning should be part of your routine.

Regular cleaning prevents the possible transmission of diseases which can be found in the fecal matter of reptiles, and which may be transmissible to humans. Not only will this keep the interior of the enclosure clean, odor-free, and healthy, but it will also keep you and your family safe and healthy.

Spot cleaning the interior of the cage should be done as often as possible – at least once a day or once every other day. When you spot clean your snake's enclosure, you should make sure that any fecal matter is removed (or as soon as you see them), the shedded skin is removed as well as the uneaten or left over food. The water bowls should also be replaced more than once a week to prevent bacterial growth.

Guidelines on How to Clean Your Snake's Enclosure

During the cleaning process, you will need to relocate the snake so that you can clean and sterilize the entire cage components, including perches, decorations, substrate, etc. To be able to do this thoroughly, you will need to temporarily relocate your Gopher Snake to a different holding cage or cell. As usual, make sure that this cage is secure and clean, and is sufficiently ventilated.

Before doing a full cleanse of your Gopher snake's cage, you must first find a suitable temporary cage for your snake. Check for components you need to clean and replace such as the bedding of the cage. After doing these, you may start cleaning by following these steps:

Step 1: Gather your cleaning materials. Grab paper towels, spray disinfectant, water sprayer, trash bag, spray bottle, brushes, buckets, sponges, gloves and other materials you think will come in handy.

Step 2: Relocate your Gopher snake to a temporary cage. A medium-sized tank with a lid and air holes will do or another smaller.

Step 3: Unplug all the electrical devices on the cage. This includes your basking lamp and under tank heater or other heat source. Remove your gauges or thermometers as well.

Step 4: Remove all the cage furniture items and decorations. Water bowls, hides, branches, rocks, plants and substrate. You can place them in the bathtub or sink where you'll wash them. You can also replace old substrate with new bedding. If your bedding of choice is shavings or coconut fiber and the likes, you can easily dump it or use a vacuum.

Step 5: Clean the empty cage. Use a spray bottle with water and paper towels to clear the dust, feces, and other dirt. Afterwards, use an antibacterial disinfectant.

Step 6: Leave the cage open and let it dry. You can also wipe the glasses clean with a soft cloth or rug so it can finish drying completely while you clean the other items.

Step 7: Clean the cage items with antibacterial soap and hot water. You may soak some items overnight in a diluted bleach solution if you have difficulty getting the dirt out. Do not scrub plastic bowls with fingernails or scouring pads. It will leave scratches on the bowl and it will make it harder to clean in the future. Instead, use the smooth part of your finger to rub the bowl clean, or soak it overnight.

Step 8: Make sure to clean the water bowl. Rinse it with hot water thoroughly with antibacterial soap and hot water. You can also use water cleaner that you can purchase from pet stores to make sure that your water is safe for your snake.

Step 9: Add new bedding and replace the furniture (optional). Or you can just return the materials you cleaned in the cage. Don't forget to fill up the bowl with fresh water.

Step 10: Put your snake back in and plug in the electrical devices. Make sure all the locks and latches are secure, and clean up your separate tank or the temporary cage as well.

Husbandry Tips

- Feed your snakes alone to avoid food aggression if in case you have other snakes inside the cage.

- Be sure to stay away from your snake until the lump from the prey disappears.

- Provide fresh water. Use a relatively deep bowl, check the water bowl every day and always keep it clean. If the Gopher Snake starts to feel very moist, take the water bowl out and return it for a few days every week.

- Handle your snake gently. Keep in mind that this is a wild animal, so it may be afraid of you for quite some time. Gently hold your snake and stay away from its face, especially at first.

- Watch out for shedding. Never handle your snake when you think it's getting ready to shed. Don't bother them at this point until they completely get out of their old skin.

- Don't restrain your snake. Gopher snakes almost never bite, restraining them will make them feel threatened and become aggressive. Don't also squeeze them too hard; just let them flow gently through your hands and fingers.

- Make sure your snake's vivarium is of a suitable size, has a correct cage temperature, maintain scrupulous hygiene, provide environmental enrichment, handle your Gopher snake regularly and carefully and of course, avoid stressing them out.

Illnesses caused by Unsanitary Living Condition

- Find a vet who is a snake expert. You may have to travel to find a competent vet since most vets don't come in contact with snakes that often which is why it is a great idea to get connected with one before anything goes wrong.

- Watch for mites because mites love to live on Gopher snakes. Keep an eye out especially around their mouth, eyes, and under their scales. If ever your snake becomes lethargic or not eating, this might be caused by mites so always give them an inspection.

- Gopher snake that makes wheezing may have a respiratory infection that may be caused by an unsanitary enclosure, improper temperature or it has come in contact with a snake that is infected. In some cases, Gopher snake will need an antibiotic so it's better to consult your veterinarian.

- Pay attention to regurgitation because it's not unusual for Gopher snakes to regurgitate after eating but since this may be a sign of serious illness, you should keep an eye on your pet for other symptoms if you see them do this. If it always happens, your snake will eventually start to lose weight, as soon as you notice these signs; do not hesitate to take it to the vet immediately.

Chapter Seven: Dealing and Handling Your Gopher Snakes

Some Gopher snake species are easy to deal with when it comes to feeding them. However, there are still some species out there that might be a bit aggressive so it's important that you also learn on how to socialize and tame these pets if ever they get defensive. This chapter will teach you some basic handling skills, how to feed them especially on their first few days, and some frequently ask questions about taming aggressive behavior of snakes just in case your pet will have trouble adjusting with its new environment.

Dealing with Your Gopher Snake

Dealing with your new snake is not hard but it will definitely take some time, whether it's a hatchling or captive-bred Gopher snake might show a little aggression or with a great deal of aggressive behavior. The first thing you should consider is to allow your Gopher snake to adjust to you. It is normal for them to hide or defend themselves, but they cannot really harm you.

What you need to do as soon as your snake arrives like in the first few days or week is to just let it sit outside its terrarium for about an hour each day and allow it to get used to your smell. Never attempt to touch your Gopher snake during these first few weeks. Give your new pet a few weeks to settle into its home and get used to a regular feeding routine. Remember, snakes are also living beings that need to settle and get used to new spaces.

Your snake may take some time getting used to you, so try not to stress it out with unnecessary handling. At the end of this initial week, you can now begin to move things around inside your Gopher snake's terrarium. However, it is still not allowed to attempt to touch your Gopher snake at this point. Continuously do this for another week so that your Gopher snake can get used to the idea that you have no intention to harm him. Being around it without attempting to touch it will let your Gopher snake know that you are not a danger or threat.

Once you think that your snake know that you are not a threat, you can start to touch it while inside its cage by placing your hand in its cage and gently start touching it, moving it around inside the cage, and lifting your snake's tail. Continue doing this manner to your snake for three to four days.

Once you see that your pet is comfortable with its new surroundings, you can start approaching your snake. Start handling it for short periods. However, do not handle it for the first two to three days after a meal. Approach your Gopher snake from the side to avoid threatening it as a predator would approach it from the top. Gently but confidently lift it. Hesitation will scare your Gopher snake and will cause it to hide or bite. When your Gopher snake realizes you are not going to eat it, it will calm down and tame quickly. Eventually, it will become used to handling.

It is also ideal to handle your Gopher snake under the supervision of a professional or long-time keeper before actually getting one for yourself. This will guarantee that you are comfortable with your pet snake when you get it.

Taming Your Gopher Snake

If you acquire an adult Gopher snake, you'll need to most likely tame it because first of all, the snake didn't grew up with you, doesn't know your smell, and since it doesn't recognize you it may become aggressive and feel threatened.

Know why your Gopher snake is aggressive

The first thing to do is to know what type of aggression your Gopher snake is showing. There are two types of aggressive responses you can de-program your Gopher snake. It can either be territorial or defensive responses and feeding responses.

Territorial or Defensive Responses

This are instinctive and not an expression of aggressions. Snakes live most of their lives in fear, since they are always being preyed at by some bigger creatures, including humans, so this kind of response is more of a defense mechanism which can be tamed with gentle and consistent care.

Feeding Responses

Feeding responses are also a natural and instinctive response. Generally, snakes are biologically programed to bite whatever comes into their terrarium. Since they assume that anything that comes to their cage is food, you might get bitten if you put your hand inside without first deprogramming this aggressive response.

FAQs on How to Handle and Tame Your Snake

Why is my Gopher snake aggressive and what can I do?
Some species of Gopher snake are more aggressive than others and might be requiring more training. If you're dealing with a particularly aggressive type of Gopher snake, you might consider training it by using a hook. You can do this by gently rubbing its body or pushing down on its head with a hook or a similar inanimate object, every time you go to get it out of its cage. By doing this, your Gopher snake will be able to know it is not yet feeding time so there is no need to bite whatever enters its terrarium.

My snake looks scared, what should I do to calm them down?
If your Gopher snake appears to be scared whenever you open its terrarium, spend a little more time rubbing its body with the hook until it calms down. If your snake coils into a ball, flatten out its body or pose a striking position, spend some time rubbing its body until it comes to a point that it will relax a bit. Start rubbing your Gopher snake's body down from its tail end and up to its head. It could seem

threatening if you start it with its head especially if your snake is already scared.

How do I handle a Feeding Response aggression?

People get bitten by their pet snake mostly because their snake is reacting to its feeding response every time something enters its terrarium. To handle this kind of response, stop feeding your Gopher snake every week. Instead, feed it only once every three weeks, but be sure to handle your snake every day. This will deprogram your Gopher snake from thinking that everything that enters its terrarium is food. It can also be useful to feed your snake in a separate tub. This will also help it from thinking that everything that comes to its terrarium is food. But don't feed it only in the tub because this will just transfer its response from the terrarium to the tub.

Why should I wash my hands before handling my snake?

You should always wash your hands thoroughly before handling your Gopher snake. Snakes have an excellent sensory organ so if they smell a scent of prey on your hand, your Gopher snake might mistake your hand for something it should eat. Also, washing your hands before handling your Gopher snake helps prevent any foreign bacteria, germs, or parasites in your pet's environment.

How can I properly pick up my pet when I'm handling it?

It is very vital to support your Gopher snake's body when you are picking or handling it up so that it is comfortable with you and there is no strain put on its body. This is true whether you are picking your Gopher snake up with your hands or with a hook. Keep the first third of your snake's body supported with either the hook or one of your hands, while supporting the back two thirds of your Gopher snake body with your other arm. Keep in mind your hook training before putting your hands in your terrarium. Lightly pressing down on your Gopher snake's head with a hook will give the snake an idea that it is not feeding time so there is no need to strike. Never grab your Gopher snake by the end of its tail to pick it up or move it. This can cause serious strain and fear to your pet.

I'm scared of its head, how can I make sure I'm safe?
Until you know within yourself that you can properly handle your snake, it is a good idea to hold it with its head facing away from you. This will give your Gopher snake a chance to become familiar with the motion of your hands or body without risking to get bitten (although if you do get bitten, it's part of taking care of them, so better get used to it). Restraining your Gopher snake's head can make it believe that you are a predator that's trying to hurt the snake. Whenever you handle your Gopher snake, stick to holding it by its body, and avoid holding or restraining its head.

Should I help with its shedding process?

No! Do not handle a Gopher snake or any snake for this matter whenever they are shedding because they might be more aggressive during these times.

Chapter Eight: Breeding Your Gopher Snakes

In this chapter you'll be provided with information about how to identify the sex of your snake as well as some breeding basics like how to set up breeding conditions, its ovulation, incubation and hatching process. Before you can breed a snake though, you have to familiarize yourself with your pet, learn more about its biology, its breeding behavior and also ask help from breeders online, within your community or attend reptile conferences so that you can have knowledge on how to successfully breed them and become a reputable breeder yourself.

Sexual Dimorphism

More often than not, a determination of a snake's sex can be established from their behavior. Males are generally more active than females. They also tend to refuse food during breeding time. But perhaps the best sign that your snake is a male is when he averts his hemi-penis when he is defecating. When he sheds his skin, the hemi-penis can be identified as two dried bits of skin at the vent which should not be confused with a small bump that can also show in the shed skin of females. Their tail shape can also differ, with the male's being more parallel and bulbous, as opposed to the female's tail which is more tapered in shape.

You can find out your snake's sex by also doing two things, the first method is through cloacal popping. Cloacal popping is done by applying pressure with the thumb just below the vent. This will cause the hemi-penis of a male to avert, one on each side of the cloacal opening. Females, on the other hand, may avert her cloaca and erect her scent gland papillae.

The next method you can try is cloacal probing. It is the more commonly employed means of sexing. It is done by gently inserting a lubricated probe, which is a slender

stainless steel, into the side of the vent, and then sliding
them into the pockets that are found on either side of the tail.

For males, the probe will slide to a depth of
approximately 10 scales, while for a female, it will go for
only 3 or 4 scales. Sometimes the probe will only go
somewhere between these two ranges, and these are often
classified as unsexed snakes. Probing isn't always definitive
or certain, and other factors may influence the result such as
the pressure you exert on the probe, or something blocking
the pockets so you could not insert the probe deep enough.
It is essential that you don't try to attempt to probe your
snake if you do not have sufficient experience with sexing.

How to Set Up the Right Breeding Conditions

Breeding snakes is not as hard as it may seem but
before anything else you have to make sure that if you are
going to breed a snake, you have to get in their heads and
think about breeding in a way that a snake will think about
breeding in the environment or in the wild. You have to
learn about the conditions needed and the triggers to make
your Gopher snakes breed. So let's say for example, if these
snakes are in the wild, and there's like a drought in the
forest or there's no abundance of food, it's most likely that

these snakes will not breed because the conditions are not good, and they know that the baby snakes they will produce will not survive or have a 'good life.'

There are four things you need to keep in mind for you to be able to successfully breed your Gopher snakes should you choose to. These are conditions, food, follicle growth, and copulation. These four factors will trigger your pet snake to breed

Conditions

Living conditions refers to the right temperature and humidity. As previously mentioned, the temperature for Gopher snake should be 85 – 90 degrees F, and the cool spot side of the cage should have less than 80 degrees. To prepare your Gopher snake for breeding you can cool them down a bit by around 4 or 5 degrees at least 6 to 8 hours every day during their breeding season. Gopher snake's usually breed around the months of November to March, then you can start to warm them up. Once you have these conditions ready you can now move to checking out the follicle growth of your female Gopher snake.

Follicle Growth

You can find the follicles of your female Gopher snake just near the gallbladder. However, you may need to use an ultrasound or maybe take a trip to the vet and find out if there's any growth in its follicles. Usually if your snake's follicles measure about 10 -12 millimeters that could be a good starting point for breeding, although it may be different for other snake species but it is usually the average size that you need. These follicles are a sign that your female is ready for breeding.

If you don't have an ultrasound or going to the vet may seem costly, what you can do to measure the snake's follicle is through feeling the bumps on your snake's body. Its follicles are located about two – thirds down the body almost before its tail. What you can do is get your Gopher snake out of the cage, and then have her go back inside the enclosure while holding her and letting their body run through your fingers. You can also tickle their tail a little bit to get her going inside. However, do not rub or slide your fingers down its body because you're not going to feel anything. What you should do is to just let her crawl through your hand, while pinching your fingers in its body a little bit so you can feel the follicle bumps.

Copulation

Once you get the conditions right and hit the right number of follicle measurement, which means you can start breeding them or copulating them with a male snake at least every 3 to 4 weeks but be sure to let them rest after a few weeks of copulation. You can start copulating it again once its follicles hits 20 mm, and just pretty much have it continuously bred every 3 – 4 weeks until the follicle hits 30 mm. When it does, you can check it again using an ultrasound to see if she is beginning to ovulate. If the follicles measure around 35 – 40 mm that means that your female snake will start its ovulation process in probably about 2 weeks or so. You can copulate your male and female snake for about 3 to 5 times for better chances of reproducing babies.

Food

Once your female snake's follicles measures about 20 – 22 mm or around the second or third time of its copulation, you'll notice the female snakes will go off of food, and it will eventually grow the follicles without food. Within a couple days of your female snake's breeding, you want to give them more food. Feed her as much as she will eat or at least more than her normal food range, say about 3 – 4 medium – size fuzzies or thawed food, though she may only eat two or three, they'll also eventually stop eating on their own.

Ovulation and Laying

When all of these trigger factors are achieved, the condition, the food, the copulation, and follicle growth that will make your female snake ovulate and produce babies because they'll know that the conditions are perfect, and there's an abundance of food which means that their babies will survive and have an awesome life. For a breeding pair, females should ideally be bigger and heavier than males. This is to allow them to have sufficient body weight that can undergo the stress of egg production. Females are usually paired only after they have reached 3 or 4 years old. Males, on the other hand, can be a lot younger and lighter; some use males that have reached 50 to 700 grams. The selected breeding pair must both be in good health, with good body weight and muscle tone.

Once the Gopher snake completes its ovulation process, it will eventually lay eggs so it's very important that there will be an incubation area and a laying area which is very easy to do. You can use different kinds of mosses so they can burrow down in the vermiculite. You have to take note that the substrate should stay damp but not wet. You'll get hatchlings quicker at higher temperatures but you will also get more congenital defects. Those defects normally show up not only in immune problems, but in different patterns of color.

Incubation and Hatching of Eggs

Incubation for baby Gopher snakes should be at 80 - 85 degrees and 55 - 60% humidity after 65 to 75 days or about 10 weeks. Female Gopher snakes will typically lay 12 to 14 oblong or elliptical eggs that are leathery in texture. Upon hatching, the baby Gopher snakes will measure 20 to 46 centimeters and will eat pink mice after their first shed, within three to seven days of hatching. Caring for baby Gopher snakes is the same as for adults, but you must also pay close attention to keep them from escaping. You must also feed them smaller fuzzies more frequently. As the snake gets bigger, feed them larger fuzzies until they can finally eat what a normal adult Gopher snake eats.

Successful Breeding

If you want to be successful in breeding your Gopher snakes or you want to become a reputable breeder someday, you have to be diligent when it comes to breeding them, and not just breed them for breeding's sake. Make sure that you also 'read' your pet by paying attention to its behavior so you can ensure that you are doing what they want to do or how they want to behave in certain conditions like breeding. And the most important thing is to have a good time when you're breeding them.

Life Cycle of a Snake

Just after copulation or the mating process, the female snake will begin to ovulate, and then she will store the sperm eggs into its oviduct for around two months to get it fertilized. After being fertilized, the female snake will eventually lay those eggs usually in shallow holes or under the ground/substrate. The mother snake will now begin looking after its eggs until those eggs hatch. The eggs' shell has a soft and leathery texture, and it's not a hard shell. For those who are breeding captive snakes, you can help it hatch by putting it under proper lighting or heating temperature (consult other breeders or your vet for the proper temperature for that particular snake species).

The snakelet or young snake will obtain its food from the egg yolk until it comes out of the shell. Once the incubation period is done, the snakelet will bite the egg of its shell, and start eating thawed food from then on and also begin shedding. Juvenile snakes will reach sexual maturity around 2 – 4 years (depending on the snake species), and usually molts or sheds skin more than thrice in a year. Once these adult snakes were again bred to other snake species, the life cycle will start again.

Chapter Nine: Common Diseases and Treatments for Gopher Snakes

Snakes are the kind of creatures that are both predators and preys in the wild, which is why they don't often show any sign of weakness because they might get preyed on by other larger animals. You may not notice any signs that your pet Gopher snake is ill unless you regularly check on it and also learn the subtle symptoms of common diseases so that you can prevent it and give your snake proper treatment before it's too late. In this chapter, we'll take a look at some of the minor problems of snakes as well as some common illnesses affecting Gopher snakes.

Common Health Problems

In this section, you will be provided with some of the most common health problems affecting Gopher snakes. If you are aware of the possible diseases and knows what to watch out for that could cause potential threat for your pet's health, it can save their life and also save you lots of money.

Minor Problems:

Lack of Appetite

Anorexia or lack of appetite is very common among captive Gopher snakes including other snake species and captive reptiles. However, you should keep in mind that lack of appetite is not a disease but a symptom – a potentially major sign that your pet has other health problems. Sometimes though, anorexia is just purely caused by the new living condition of your pet or a combination of lots of factors like stress, housing or living condition, type of food etc. Breeders call it the "maladaptation syndrome," and the simplest explanation for it is that your snake is having a hard time thriving in its new captive environment.

Chapter Nine: Common Diseases and Treatments for Gopher Snakes

Mostly, the main reason for a lack of appetite in captive snakes is husbandry deficiencies. This is great news because you can hopefully encourage your pet to eat eventually if you just improve their living condition or learn how they've lived before from their previous breeders or study what they are like in the wild so you can adjust to their needs accordingly.

You must be able to do some adjustments within the enclosure, the materials, hiding spots, water dishes as well as other important factors like the temperature, humidity levels and probably the food itself. Make sure that the kind of food you feed them is appropriate for their breed, age, and size. The frequency of feeding also matters.

If you think that the housing or the living condition is not the problem, then another potential cause of anorexia is an underlying disease or other medical issues. It can either be from trauma (transferring to a new home, sudden change of environment), metabolic/ organic causes (kidney, liver or respiratory problems), and parasites or other infectious disease. If that happens, your pet snake may eventually suffer from a broken jaw since it is not eating or refuses to eat.

If you found out that the lack of appetite is caused by serious internal problems, you should take your pet to the vet immediately so that he'll be given proper treatment. On the other hand, if the animal is just adjusting to its new environment or it's only because of failing to thrive, then nutritional support and proper living condition is necessary to help your pet overcome or recover from this illness. If ever you're thinking that feeding your snake enough calories through force feeding them will make this problem go away or this symptom to stop – it won't. Address this problem by going to the vet to find out the real cause of its lack of appetite so that you'll snake will completely recovered from it.

Vomiting and Regurgitation

Regurgitation or vomiting is another common condition suffered by snakes that is also related to anorexia. The difference between vomiting and regurgitation is that the former expels the food from the gastrointestinal tract just right below the stomach while the latter expels the food above the stomach or from the stomach itself. It may seem insignificant but it all makes a huge difference from a medical point of view.

The major causes for vomiting or regurgitation are again husbandry problems and improper handling. If the temperature inside the enclosure is too low it or if these snakes are being handled right after eating it will cause them to either vomit or regurgitate.

These problems are fortunately very easy to treat, just like in anorexia, you may just need to examine your management or husbandry practices to find out what causes inconvenience to your snake and prompt them this symptom. However, if the living condition is not the problem, it only means that there are much worse causes like bacteria, fungi, parasites, viruses or other serious diseases in the kidney, pancreas, liver, and even its brain.

One way of finding out if your snake has serious problems that causes the vomiting or regurgitation is to have a routine fecal sample, lab tests, and MRI, though it can be very expensive which is why saving up ahead of time for emergency costs can come in handy. It may be wise to bring your snake to the vet for a routine physical examination especially if it's a new pet.

Major Problems:

Acariasis

Acariasis is a mites and ticks infestation among snakes. This don't just affect one snake, it could also affect other snake species if ever you have more than one, and it can also be associated with other illnesses. The ectoparasites should be identified immediately so that proper treatment can be given.

The most common type of snake mite that causes Acariasis in snake is called *Ophionyssus natricis*. These adult mites sucks blood from its host, and can be potentially life – threatening if there's already a swarm of mites in your snake which will eventually lead to anemia. Aside from that, these mites can also transfer a disease from one animal species to another, making the problem even worse.

Acariasis is mainly because of unsanitary living conditions, imports, and improper husbandry. Mites can usually be found on pets imported from other countries that are not properly quarantined or may not be quarantined at all. This will cause mites to spread in the whole collection and transfer from one species to another. If you are acquiring a snake from other countries, you have to make sure that it is properly quarantined, otherwise you will risk the lives of your other snakes or other reptile collections if any. Snake mites also serve as vectors for other disease causing agents like *Aeromonas hydrophila* (a bacteria that causes pneumonia and infectious stomatitis), Leukocytozoon and other hematozoans.

Mites could just be found under the skin of your snake's jaw or it covers your snake's skin, and worse its entire body. You can perhaps easily notice it because they are a collection, it also varies on colors, age and how it has taken a blood meal off your pet.

If you notice your pet snake having a lack – luster or sort of bland appearance it might already be infested with mites. You should check its chin/gular folds, scutes, periocular areas around its eyes, and the skin around its cloaca (reproductive organ) because this is where most mites accumulate. If you have a large pet collection, mites or Ectoparasites could be difficult to remove. They are a source of further disease but if you diagnosed it as soon as possible, it can be given proper treatment and eventually be exterminated from your pet. Make sure that even after your snake is free of these mites or ticks, you have to clean and thoroughly treat the entire enclosure, collection or cage. If the environment is not properly cleaned or treated, mites can potentially accumulate and infest your snake/s again.

Pneumonia

Pneumonia is caused by several respiratory factors like nasal discharge, virus and other ailments associated with the nasal cavity, lungs and breathing. Pneumonia is a very subtle and deadly disease among snakes because often times, its symptoms are unnoticeable and when owners get to notice them, the disease is already advance and difficult to treat.

The most common symptom you should look out for is a nasal discharge. Nasal discharge could mean that your snake may only have problems in its upper lungs, which can be easily treated with antibiotics. However, this can also be a sign of an advanced pneumonia affecting the lower lungs of your snake. Respiratory infections that affect the nostrils, trachea, lungs, and air sacs can mean a severe case. Snakes can't cough because they lack a diaphragm so if ever their respiratory tract gets filled up with pus fluids and the likes, they'll have difficulty in breathing. If you notice that your snake prop itself in its enclosure with its head and neck held up, and opens its mouth it only means that he has difficulty in breathing, and only gravity is keeping the pulmonary fluid in a portion of the lungs so that the snake will be able to partially breathe. Pneumonia and other respiratory problems are often caused by poor husbandry because if the snake is not housed in a preffered optimal temperature environment it can become stress, weaken the immune system, and predisposes the snake in various diseases.

A strong immune system is needed to attack various infections like viruses, parasites, and bacteria so that it will not progress into major illnesses. Another major factor of respiratory illnesses is humidity. If a desert snake species like the Gopher snake is placed in a highly humid condition it won't have the ability to adjust with the excess water in its lungs. This is also true for other snake species that tolerates high – humidity environment but are placed in a very dry condition. The mucous will dry up in the lungs which will eventually cause infections. Nutrition is another factor; lack of Vitamin A can cause serious respiratory problems.

The treatment for bacterial infections and viruses that causes respiratory problems is usually antibiotics, but it only treats secondary infections, and not the root cause of the problem. If the snake has a refractory respiratory disease, he will need a thorough lab examination to pinpoint the cause. Tests like bacterial culture, pulmonary washes, X – rays, cytology and sensitivity testing are usually being done to snakes with possible respiratory conditions. Advanced pneumonia are usually examined by using an MRI, endoscopy, CT – scan, various blood tests, and viral screening. Pneumonia results to high mortality among snakes.

Chapter Ten: Care Sheet and Summary

This chapter will give you a quick summary of all the essential things you need to remember when it comes to taking care of your pet Gopher snake. Keep in mind that lots of factors are involved to become a good breeder or keeper. You need to make sure that the snake your getting is healthy, and the breeder it came from is reputable or responsible, you also need to feed it properly, follow good husbandry practices, and provide all its needs especially its housing conditions because it can ultimately save your snake from harmful and potentially serious illnesses. Having a pet snake could be an awesome experience if you learn how to deal with them and value them.

Biological Information

Taxonomy: *Pituophis catenifer catenifer*. They belong in Kingdom *Animalia*, Phylum *Chordata*, Class *Reptilia*, Order *Squamata*, Family *Colubridae*, Genus *Pituophis*, and Species *P. catenifer*.

Country of Origin: North America, Mexico, Canada Common Areas: lowlands, shrublands, woodlands, desert, coniferous forest, farmland, marshes, coastal grasslands, and also prairies

Size: 4 - 7 feet long; 36 - 96 inches

Body Type and Appearance: Has big eyes with rounded pupils with a large head but narrow necks. Usually have dark stripes on top of its head

Color: Have brown or reddish color blotches on its back, and its ground color is yellow, straw, tan or cream color. There are also smaller blotches found on its side. A dark strip runs in front of its eye to the angle of its jaw.

Defense Mechanism: When threatened the Gopher snake prepares for a striking position by lowering its head, hissing loudly, and shaking its tail. This defensive behavior along with its body markings frequently caused the Gopher snake to be mistaken for a Rattlesnake.

Sub – Species of Gopher Snakes:

Sonoran Gopher Snake -Has reddish – brown dorsal blotches in its saddle; has darkish brown or black colors on its tail

San Diego Gopher Snake - A huge snake with lots of keeled scales; its head is wider than the neck, and has a rounded snout.

Pacific Gopher Snake - Its body has no blotches, but it has stripes with a tan or straw ground color.

Great Basin Gopher Snake - Great Basin Gopher snakes have dorsal markings that are dark brown or black in color.

Bullsnake - Bull snakes have brownish or yellowish dorsal blotches, and typically have smaller dark spots on its side, its head is also narrow.

Lifespan: 12 - 15 years on average; 33 longest recorded lifespan

Gopher Snakes as Pets

Temperament: Gopher snakes are generally docile species, but for some of its sub – species they tend to become aggressive when threatened, especially if you caught it in the wild or have not had proper socialization and taming. Gopher snakes are very active during day time and are also very curious of its surrounding which is why you need to provide adequate space for it to freely move around.

Other pets: All reptile and snake species for this matter are carnivorous and natural predators. Make sure that you keep them away from your pet snake or provide a secured enclosure so that your Gopher will not slip away.

Major Pro: non – venomous, suited for novice keepers, generally docile and easy to tame, curious and active, very easy to feed, does not neglect any food compared to other snake species.

Major Con: Growth may be quite hard to manage since it can get as long as 7 feet; some sub – species like the Sonora Gopher snake and/or Bull Snakes are quite aggressive, and may not be ideal as pets, though some owners have properly tamed it.

Legal Requirements and Snake Licensing:

- You don't need a license to keep Gopher snakes since they are non – venomous which means that even if they bite a human or a stranger, it will not kill them.
- Make sure that you ask first your local and state laws and an ordinance, to see what is permitted and what is not.

- It is necessary for importing, exporting, or traveling with an exotic or a naturally dangerous animal. There may be special laws about bringing your pet with you to other countries especially in United Kingdom or Asia.
- Make sure to research thoroughly about how to bring your pet snake to another country, and the specific laws that apply depending on what part of the region or place you will stay.

Habitat Requirements for Gopher Snakes: Glass Enclosure with a screen top or lid; Bedding or Substrate; Water Dish; Under Tank Heater; Basking Lamp; Heat and Water Temperature Regulator/ Gauges; Hiding Place and other decor materials

Purchasing and Selecting a Healthy Breed

Where to Purchase: Reptile Shops, Private Breeders, Reptile Shows, Rescue Centers

Characteristics of a Reputable Breeder:

- Good breeders must be knowledgeable about the breeds they raise, and should give you specific info about the breed.

- They should be able to teach you how to properly set up the enclosure, where to place it, and the right temperature/humidity levels needed.

- Good breeders will walk you through every step of the process. They are willing to answer all of your questions and if they think that you are not a good fit as an owner, they won't sell it to you.

Characteristics of a Healthy Breed: Look out for is the eyes; you want to look for clear eyes that are free of any discharge; next is the breathing - you need to look out for a healthy breathing with no signs of labor breathing, and no nostril discharge. You should also opt to get a snake that has a rounded and full body, and a species that is active and alert to its environment. It should not have any mobility issues, the snake should be able to move freely as well.

Habitat Requirements for Gopher Snakes:

How to Set Up Habitat for Your Snake:

Step 1: Purchase a 20 – gallon tank for your Gopher snake or maybe something a little bit bigger

Step 2: Assign a space for a basking area, and a space for a normal temperature where your snake can rest and coil up so that you'll know where to properly put the materials you bought.

Step 3: Provide inside a cage is the bedding and/or substrate

Step 4: Place the cage materials like water bowls/water dish, some plants, perches, and your snake's hiding spot but before you do make sure to determine the right size you'll need for your pet.

Step 5: Set up the under tank heater, the basking lamp, and also attach a heat and humidity gauges.

Regulating Temperature

- The temperature for Gopher snakes should be 85 – 90 degrees Fahrenheit
- Provide basking lamp or overheat lamp that has like a UVB light, put it on top of the cage's lid or on the side to help warm up that side of the cage especially during cold season. Remember that the basking area should cover about less than half of the cage, and the cooler side should have a temperature that is less than 80 degrees Fahrenheit.
- Water bowls should also be located on the cooler side and not on the basking area.

- Attach an analog thermometer to regulate the cage's temperature.

Nutritional Requirements

In the wild: Gopher snakes are mainly carnivores who like to eat mammals particularly gophers, squirrels, rodents, rabbits and birds found in the forest and underneath the ground.

In captivity: the best food you can feed them are fuzzies or thawed mice which are frozen and easy to buy, though you may need to serve it a bit warm to your snake.

Feeding Conditions: Be sure to set up and stabilize their habitat before bringing your Gopher snake home so they can also digest and absorb food properly

Feeding Amount/Frequency: They only need to be fed about once a week or in ten days. You can choose to feed your adult Gopher snake with a squirrel that is about the size of the rodent.

How to Feed Gopher Snake:

- If you feed your Gopher Snake, don't handle it for at least 24 hours after feeding the snake. Give them time to digest their food because it is not a good idea if you handle it straight after you feed it.

- Increase the size of the rodent appropriately as your snake grows.

- Take into account of using tongs when feeding your Gopher snake to avoid accidental bites.

Maintenance for Gopher Snakes

Spot Cleaning Your Snake's Enclosure:

- Spot cleaning the interior of the cage should be done as often as possible – at least once a day or once every other day.
- You should make sure that any fecal matter is removed (or as soon as you see them), the shedded skin is removed as well as the uneaten or left over food.
- The water bowls should also be replaced more than once a week to prevent bacterial growth.

Guidelines on How to Clean Your Snake's Enclosure

Step 1: Gather your cleaning materials

Step 2: Relocate your Gopher snake to a temporary cage.

Step 3: Unplug all the electrical devices on the cage.

Step 4: Remove all the cage furniture items and decorations.

Step 5: Clean the empty cage.

Step 6: Leave the cage open and let it dry.

Step 7: Clean the cage items with antibacterial soap and hot water.

Step 8: Make sure to clean the water bowl.

Step 9: Add new bedding and replace the furniture (optional).

Step 10: Put your snake back in and plug in the electrical devices.

Dealing and Handling Your Gopher Snakes

- Never attempt to touch your Gopher snake during these first few weeks. Give your new pet a few weeks to settle into its home and get used to a regular feeding routine.
- At the end of this initial week, you can now begin to move things around inside your Gopher snake's terrarium.
- Approach your Gopher snake from the side to avoid threatening it as a predator would approach it from the top.

Taming Your Snake

- Know why your Gopher snake is aggressive either from territorial /defensive responses or feeding responses

Territorial/Defensive Responses: You can hook train them, and spend a little more time rubbing its body with the hook until it calms down.

Feeding Responses: To handle this kind of response, stop feeding your Gopher snake every week. Instead, feed it only once every three weeks, but be sure to handle your snake every day

Breeding Your Gopher Snakes

Sexual Dimorphism: Males are generally more active than females. They also tend to refuse food during breeding time. But perhaps the best sign that your snake is a male is when he averts his hemi-penis when he is defecating.

How to Set Up the Right Breeding Conditions:

Temperature: The temperature for Gopher snake should be 85 – 90 degrees F, and the cool spot side of the cage should have less than 80 degrees. To prepare your Gopher snake for breeding you can cool them down a bit by around 4 or 5

degrees at least 6 to 8 hours every day during their breeding season.

Follicle Growth: Usually if your snake's follicles measure about 10 -12 millimeters that could be a good starting point for breeding. What you should do is to just let her crawl through your hand, while pinching your fingers in its body a little bit so you can feel the follicle bumps.

Copulation: You can start breeding them or copulating them with a male snake at least every 3 to 4 weeks but be sure to let them rest after a few weeks of copulation. You can start copulating it again once its follicles hits 20 mm, and just pretty much have it continuously bred every 3 – 4 weeks until the follicle hits 30 mm.

Food: Feed her as much as she will eat or at least more than her normal food range, say about 3 – 4 medium – size fuzzies or thawed food

Sexual Maturity: 2 - 4 years
Incubation Period: 65 to 75 days or about 10 weeks
Litter Size: 12 to 14 oblong or elliptical eggs that are leathery in texture
Size of baby Gopher snakes: 20 to 46 centimeters

Common Diseases and Health Requirements

Minor Diseases: Anorexia or Lack of Appetite, Vomiting and Regurgitation

Major Diseases: Acariasis and Pneumonia

Glossary of Snake Terms

1.2.3. (Numbers with full stops) – The numbers are used to denote the number of a species, arranged according to sex, thus: male.female.unknown sex. In this case, one male, two females, and three of unknown sex.

Acclimation – Adjusting to a new environment or new conditions over a period of time.

Active range – The area of activity which can include hunting, seeking refuge, and finding a mate.

Ambient temperature – The overall temperature of the environment.

Amelanistic – Amel for short; without melanin, or without any black or brown coloration.

Anal Plate – A modified ventral scale that covers and protects the vent; sometimes a single plate, sometimes a divided plate.

Anerythristic – Anery for short; without any red coloration.

Aquatic – Lives in water.

Arboreal – Lives in trees.

Betadine – An antiseptic that can be used to clean wounds in reptiles.

Bilateral – Where stripes, spots or markings are present on both sides of an animal.

Biotic – The living components of an environment.

Brille – A transparent scale above the eyes of snakes that allows them to see but also serves to protect the eyes at the same time. Also called Spectacle, and Ocular Scale.

Brumation – The equivalent of mammalian hibernation among reptiles.

Cannibalistic – Where an animal feeds on others of its own kind.

Caudocephalic Waves – The ripple-like contractions that move from the rear to the front of a snake's body.

CB – Captive Bred, or bred in captivity.

CH – Captive Hatched.

Cloaca – also Vent; a half-moon shaped opening for digestive waste disposal and sexual organs.

Cloacal Gaping – Indication of sexual receptivity of the female.

Cloacal Gland – A gland at the base of the tail which emits foul smelling liquid as a defense mechanism; also called Anal Gland.

Clutch – A batch of eggs.

Constriction – The act of wrapping or coiling around a prey to subdue and kill it prior to eating.

Crepuscular – Active at twilight, usually from dusk to dawn.

Crypsis – Camouflage or concealing.

Diurnal – Active by day

Drop – To lay eggs or to bear live young.

Ectothermic – Cold-blooded. An animal that cannot regulate its own body temperature, but sources body heat from the surroundings.

Endemic – Indigenous to a specific region or area.

Estivation – Also Aestivation; a period of dormancy that usually occurs during the hot or dry seasons in order to escape the heat or to remain hydrated.

Faunarium (Faun) – A plastic enclosure with an air holed lid, usually used for small animals such as hatchling snakes, lizards, and insects.

FK – Fresh Killed; a term usually used when feeding a rodent that is recently killed, and therefore still warm, to a pet snake.

Flexarium – A reptile enclosure that is mostly made from mesh screening, for species that require plenty of ventilation.

Fossorial – A burrowing species.

Fuzzy – For rodent prey, one that has just reached the stage of development where fur is starting to grow.

F/T – Frozen/thawed; used to refer to food items that are frozen but thawed before feeding to your pet.

Gestation – The period of development of an embryo within a female.

Gravid – The equivalent of pregnant in reptiles.

Glottis – A tube-like structure that projects from the lower jaw of a snake to facilitate ingestion of large food items.

Gut-loading – Feeding insects within 24 hours to a prey before they are fed to your pet, so that they pass on the nutritional benefits.

Hatchling – A newly hatched, or baby, reptile.

Hemipenes – Dual sex organs; common among male snakes.

Hemipenis – A single protrusion of a paired sexual organ; one half is used during copulation.

Herps/Herpetiles – A collective name for reptile and amphibian species.

Herpetoculturist – A person who keeps and breeds reptiles in captivity.

Herpetologist – A person who studies ectothermic animals, sometimes also used for those who keeps reptiles.

Herpetology – The study of reptiles and amphibians.

Hide Box – A furnishing within a reptile cage that gives the animal a secure place to hide.

Hots – Venomous.

Husbandry – The daily care of a pet reptile.

Hygrometer – Used to measure humidity.

Impaction – A blockage in the digestive tract due to the swallowing of an object that cannot be digested or broken down.

Incubate – Maintaining eggs in conditions favorable for development and hatching.

Interstitial – The skin between scales.

Intromission – Also mating; when the male's hemipenis is inserted into the cloaca of the female.

Juvenile – Not yet adult; not of breedable age.

LTC – Long Term Captive; or one that has been in captivity for more than six months.

MBD – Metabolic Bone Disease; occurs when reptiles lack sufficient calcium in their diet.

Morph – Color pattern

Musking – Secretion of a foul smelling liquid from its vent as a defense mechanism.

Oviparous – Egg-bearing.

Ovoviviparous – Eggs are retained inside the female's body until they hatch.

Pinkie – Newborn rodent.

Pip – The act of a hatchling snake to cut its way out of the egg using a special egg tooth.

PK – Pre-killed; a term used when live rodents are not fed to a snake.

Popping – The process by which the sex is determined among hatchlings.

Probing – The process by which the sex is determined among adults.

Regurgitation – Also Regurge; occurs when a snake regurgitates or brings out a half-digested meal.

R.I. – Respiratory Infection; common condition among reptiles kept in poor conditions.

Serpentine Locomotion – The manner in which snakes move.

Sloughing – Shedding.

Sub-adult – Juvenile.

Substrate – The material lining the bottom of a reptile enclosure.

Stat – Short for Thermostat

Tag – Slang for a bite or being bitten

Terrarium – A reptile enclosure.

Thermo-regulation – The process by which cold-blooded animals regulate their body temperature by moving from hot to cold surroundings.

Vent – Cloaca

Vivarium – Glass-fronted enclosure

Viviparous – Gives birth to live young.

WC – Wild Caught.

Weaner – A sub-adult rodent.

WF – Wild Farmed; refers to the collection of a pregnant female whose eggs or young were hatched or born in captivity.

Yearling – A year old.

Zoonosis – A disease that can be passed from animal to man.

Index

C

D

E

F

G

H

I

M

N

O

P

R

S

T

U

V

W

Y

Photo Credits

Page 1 Photo by user Greg Schechter via Flickr.com, https://www.flickr.com/photos/gregthebusker/8038079283/

Page 3 Photo by user Wildlife Wanderer via Flickr.com, https://www.flickr.com/photos/wildlifewanderer/9248072205/

Page 12 Photo by user ap2il via Flickr.com, https://www.flickr.com/photos/ap2il/3439002044/

Page 28 Photo by user Nathan Rupert via Flickr.com, https://www.flickr.com/photos/nathaninsandiego/6938454621/

Page 42 Photo by user matt knoth via Flickr.com, https://www.flickr.com/photos/mattknoth/4750913500/

Page 49 Photo by user Wildlife Wanderer via Flickr.com, https://www.flickr.com/photos/wildlifewanderer/9250838882/

Page 55 Photo by user Ken Bartle via Flickr.com, https://www.flickr.com/photos/kbphoto1/7228120902/

References

"3 Stages in the Life Cycle of a Snake" Buzzle.com

http://www.buzzle.com/articles/life-cycle-of-a-snake.html

"Cleaning Your Pet Snake's Enclosure" Pets4Homes UK

https://www.pets4homes.co.uk/pet-advice/cleaning-your-pet-snakes-enclosure.html

"How to Choose a Healthy Pet Snake" AllOurPaws.com

http://allourpaws.com/reptiles/how-to-choose-a-healthy-pet-snake/

"How to Clean a Snake Cage Quickly and Easily" Reptile Knowledge

http://www.reptileknowledge.com/news/how-to-clean-a-snake-cage-quickly-and-easily/

"Gopher Snake" Nature Mapping Foundation

http://naturemappingfoundation.org/natmap/facts/gopher_snake_712.html

"Gopher Snake" Anapsid.org

http://www.anapsid.org/gopher.html

"Gopher Snakes Care – Keeping San Diego Gopher Snakes as Pets" – ReptileKnowledge.com

http://www.reptileknowledge.com/news/gopher-snakes-care-keeping-san-diego-gopher-snakes-as-pets/

"Gopher Snake Facts" – Live Science

https://www.livescience.com/53484-gopher-snake.html

"Gopher Snake Facts" – Softschools.com

http://www.softschools.com/facts/animals/gopher_snake_facts/671/

"Gopher Snakes found in California" CaliforniaHerps.com

http://www.californiaherps.com/identification/snakesid/gophersnakes.id.html

"Gopher Snake: Pituophis catenifer" Snake - Facts

http://snake-facts.weebly.com/gopher-snake.html

"Guide to Feeding a Pet Gopher Snake"
Second – Opinion – Doc.com

http://www.second-opinion-doc.com/guide-to-feeding-a-pet-gopher-snake.html

"Pituophis catenifer" Wikipedia.org

https://en.wikipedia.org/wiki/Pituophis_catenifer

"Pacific Gopher Snake" Wikipedia.org

https://en.wikipedia.org/wiki/Pacific_gopher_snake

"Pacific gopher snake breeding basics? Bull-Pine-Gopher Snakes Forum" – Repticzone.com

http://www.repticzone.com/forums/Bull-Pine-GopherSnakes/messages/2203702.html

Shocking Gopher Snake Facts You Never Knew

https://www.pestwiki.com/shocking-gopher-snake-facts/

"Snake Health 101: Common Medical Problems in Snakes" – ReptilesMagazine.com

http://www.reptilesmagazine.com/Snakes/Snake-Health-101/

"The Suitability of Gopher Snakes as Pets" Blogjob.com

https://blogjob.com/insights/2015/09/21/the-suitability-of-gopher-snakes-as-pets/

"What to consider before keeping a Gopher Snake as a pet"

Second – Opinion – Doc.com

http://www.second-opinion-doc.com/what-to-consider-before-keeping-a-gopher-snake-as-a-pet.html

Feeding Baby
Cynthia Cherry
978-1941070000

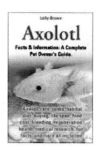

Axolotl
Lolly Brown
978-0989658430

Dysautonomia, POTS
Syndrome
Frederick Earlstein
978-0989658485

Degenerative Disc
Disease Explained
Frederick Earlstein
978-0989658485

Sinusitis, Hay Fever,
Allergic Rhinitis Explained
Frederick Earlstein
978-1941070024

Wicca
Riley Star
978-1941070130

Zombie Apocalypse
Rex Cutty
978-1941070154

Capybara
Lolly Brown
978-1941070062

Eels As Pets
Lolly Brown
978-1941070167

Scabies and Lice Explained
Frederick Earlstein
978-1941070017

Saltwater Fish As Pets
Lolly Brown
978-0989658461

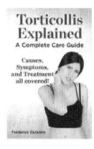

Torticollis Explained
Frederick Earlstein
978-1941070055

Kennel Cough
Lolly Brown
978-0989658409

Physiotherapist, Physical
Therapist
Christopher Wright
978-0989658492

Rats, Mice, and Dormice
As Pets
Lolly Brown
978-1941070079

Wallaby and Wallaroo Care
Lolly Brown
978-1941070031

Bodybuilding Supplements
Explained
Jon Shelton
978-1941070239

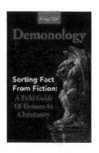

Demonology
Riley Star
978-19401070314

Pigeon Racing
Lolly Brown
978-1941070307

Dwarf Hamster
Lolly Brown
978-1941070390

Cryptozoology
Rex Cutty
978-1941070406

Eye Strain
Frederick Earlstein
978-1941070369

Inez The Miniature Elephant
Asher Ray
978-1941070353

Vampire Apocalypse
Rex Cutty
978-1941070321

Made in the USA
Las Vegas, NV
08 February 2022

43469602R00074